The Language of
The New Century Hymnal

The Language of
The New Century Hymnal

Arthur G. Clyde

WIPF & STOCK · Eugene, Oregon

Wipf and Stock Publishers
199 W 8th Ave, Suite 3
Eugene, OR 97401

The Language of the New Century Hymnal
By Clyde, Arthur G.
Copyright©1996 Pilgrim Press
ISBN 13: 978-1-60899-284-3
Publication date 11/18/2009
Previously published by Pilgrim Press, 1996

Contents

Foreword   vii

Acknowledgments   viii

The New Century Hymnal as a Resource for Our Own Time   1

The New Century Hymnal and Inclusive Language   2

The Context for the Language of a New Hymnal   3

The Process Used   7

The Theological Demands of Revising Hymns   8

Inclusive-Language Considerations in One Text   12

The Practice of Hymn Revision   14

Types of Revisions   15

Translation   15

Categories of Language Considerations   17

Archaic Language   18

Gender of God   19

Use of Father for God   21

Balancing Masculine and Feminine Images   22

Use of Mother and Other Feminine Images for God   23

Masculine Pronouns for God   24

Gender of Jesus Christ   26

Lord and Sovereign   29

Use of Lord for God   31

The Son of God, the Child of God   31

Kings, Kingdoms, and Masters   33

Militaristic Language 34

Triumphalistic Language 36

Language about the Trinity 35

Language That Includes Women, Children, and Men 38

Use of the Word "Dark" 38

Language about People's Abilities 39

Language That Recognizes Varied Human Experience 41

Language of Science and Technology 42

    Language of a Three-tiered Universe 42

    Other Language in an Age of Science and Technology 43

    Language of Domination 44

Language Other than English 44

New Hymns and New Images 45

A Word about Perfect Language 47

Appendix A: The Way It Used to Be 49

Appendix B: Hymns in Transition: "Jesus Christ Is Risen Today!" 51

Notes 53

Foreword

Language, at one and the same time, is both a means of communication and an admission that words cannot contain the full meaning of what is spoken or written. This is especially true when we "name" something or someone.

With humility, Justin Martyr, writing in about 155 C. E., begs us to remember that humankind is invited in the Genesis story of creation to name the creatures, but not God. Even Moses, at the burning bush, does not presume to name God. When asked by Moses, God gives the mysterious divine Name as "I AM THAT I AM."

This led Justin to write, "Father, and God, and Creator, and Lord, and Master are not names, but appellations derived from God's good deeds and functions."

The Language of The New Century Hymnal honors this ancient tradition of humility about all our human, transitory words for God and our culturally shaped words for ordinary speech. Our words, including the words of Holy Scripture, point to realities larger than themselves.

Where this is forgotten, words can be mistaken for the realities which they signify. This leads to an idolatry of words that is alien to the language of biblical faith. Linguistic humility is appropriate for those who follow the Word made flesh.

Thomas E. Dipko
Executive Vice President
United Church Board for Homeland Ministries

Acknowledgments

As editor of *The New Century Hymnal*, I wish to recognize the members of the editorial panel, the Hymnal Committee, and others whose names are listed in the acknowledgments of the hymnal for their work, which provided the basis for the contents of this booklet.

The New Century Hymnal as a Resource for Our Own Time

"Every generation responds to the call of Christ in its own distinctive way. There is need for periodic revision of our hymnals, none of which can contain, in any case, more than a fraction of the great store of texts and tunes available for congregational worship gathered over the centuries." These words from the introduction to the *Pilgrim Hymnal* edition of 1958 are typical of those found in many hymnals in that they recognize that each hymnal must attempt to serve the contemporary church and at the same time function as a caretaker of the hymns of the ages. *The New Century Hymnal* is published at a time of even broader challenge as the church finds itself in an age of ecumenism and amid a revival of hymn writing.

Thus a hymnal committee at this moment is given the daunting yet joyous task of presenting not only the many hymns that have served as the core of worship in the past, but also many new hymns that are in use in the ecumenical church. Moreover, this abundant list is augmented through a "hymn explosion," a great flourish of new hymns, that has taken place not only in the United States, but in many other places in the world as the church enters the twenty-first century.

The New Century Hymnal is an offering to the church of a selection of past and present for the purpose of carrying us toward the future. Its contents reflect more than rootedness in reformed hymnody. A strong commitment to ancient tradition has restored many hymn texts of the early centuries of the church. In its twentieth-century choices, a conscious effort has been made to include more hymns by women, and to recognize the increasing pluralistic nature of the church. Thus, hymns of many traditions and cultures embrace the wider family that is the church today.

Throughout the ages the psalter, which is the songbook of the Bible, has held a revered place in songs of worship. *The New Century Hymnal*, along with many denominational hymnals of this age, restores the psalms to worship in church and home, and provides ways in which the psalms can be sung.

The New Century Hymnal provides more than hymns and psalms for congregational and personal worship. It also contains the traditional orders for corporate worship taken from the *Book of Worship* of the United Church of Christ. These orders not only reflect a growing ecumenical convergence of understandings on the use of liturgy in worship, but also include texts that are widely accepted.

This liturgical renewal in the church at large has brought about the desire among leaders of worship in local churches to have more hymns for specific rites and sacraments. Consequently, the compilers of the hymnal have provided many hymns, traditional and new, for use at baptism, confirmation, and holy communion. The growing use of a common lectionary throughout many denominations has brought churches closer as the same readings are shared in Sunday worship. This has provided the opportunity for those selecting hymns to work closely with Scripture in order to find hymns related to the Bible passages that will be read in the worship service.

These are some of the main features of a book that was prepared to serve the United Church of Christ and other denominations as well. It is not only through its selection of contents, however, that this hymnal reflects the attempt to be inclusive. One of the most distinguishing aspects of *The New Century Hymnal* is its language, which is intended to include and affirm all people as children of God. That is what this booklet is about.

The New Century Hymnal and Inclusive Language

The use of inclusive language is not new to the United Church of Christ. The work that led to the publication of *The New*

Century Hymnal is rooted in actions by the General Synod of the United Church of Christ. As early as 1973, the Ninth General Synod of the denomination adopted a policy to use inclusive language in all printed materials and resources,[1] and the Eleventh General Synod in 1977 directed the Executive Council to begin to create a hymnal using language that is inclusive. The action was accompanied by other statements that called for the development of guidelines for the use of inclusive language and their implementation.[2] In 1980 the denomination's Office for Church Life and Leadership published the *Book of Worship* in inclusive language, which received wide acceptance. The United Church Board for Homeland Ministries of the United Church of Christ, at the request of General Synod, set aside funds in 1989 to take responsibility for the new hymnal project, and work was begun by a committee in 1990. This sequence gives an indication of the movement in the United Church of Christ toward the use of inclusive language in its worship life.

One of the first steps taken by the United Church Board for Homeland Ministries was an extensive research project among local churches that showed the inclusion of a large quantity of hymns, new hymns, worship resources, orders for worship, and good indexes to be of great importance. The response to this questionnaire was unusually high. For the majority of those interested in purchasing a new hymnal, inclusive language was a high priority. These findings gave support to the 1977 synod action asking for an inclusive-language hymnal.

The Context for the Language of a New Hymnal

The awareness of inclusive language in society as a whole and the experience of other denominations in dealing with worship resources, particularly hymnals, provide the starting point for the language of *The New Century Hymnal*. In society at large, people use language that attempts to show sensitivity to their neighbors. Terms such as "the deaf" and "the blind" have been replaced by "people who are deaf" and "people who are blind" in recognition that each person's humanity takes precedence over ability. Change has taken place in language intended to include both women and men. The use of "man" and "mankind" to refer to all people is falling into disuse. It is common practice to use nongendered labels for roles—firefighter, salesperson—and to search for ways of not using "he, him, his" as generic pronouns, as in "everyone to their own way." This is but a sampling of the many language issues that had to be addressed in creating a book of hymns that takes cultural change and language change seriously.

The implications of all this are both simple and complex. It cannot be assumed that the reader (and in this case, the singer in worship) possesses all the background and insights to interpret the meaning of certain words and phrases the way they were intended. That would require us all to understand and agree with the following kinds of assumptions whenever we encounter these words:

- when we say "mankind" or "men" we mean "all people"
- when we sing "wash me white as snow" we are talking only about spiritual purity and not about skin color
- whenever we say "up in heaven" we understand that heaven is not really up, but that this is an ancient understanding of the universe being arranged in three levels, a concept that we know is inconsistent with our scientific knowledge

But such language does not work in the culture of this age. All women today do not feel included in "men," even though they may be aware of its historic meaning; many people of color are offended by the phrase "wash me white" even though they understand the symbolism; and many in the scientific community are not satisfied with the persistent use of a three-tiered view of the universe that was outmoded centuries ago. Sometimes words lose their meaning, leading to misunderstandings. A child in these times who sings about "the dumb" may well be conjuring images of people who are not smart. How might a child interpret archaic language such as "If thou but suffer God to guide thee"?

Much of the archaic language in English language hymns was

written in the time period between the introduction of the King James Version of the Bible and the first part of the twentieth century. Since during this time the Scriptures were read and quoted primarily in the language of the 1611 translation under King James I of Scotland, the language of worship was cast in the same style. God is referred to as "thou" and "thee," and auxiliary verbs such as "shalt" and "wilt" are used in prayers. But in the twentieth century, revisions of the King James translation—the Revised Standard Version (RSV) in 1952, the New Revised Standard Version (NRSV) in 1989—are being used more and more. The introduction to the RSV states that the reason for the revision is "the change since 1611 in English usage." It cites the following rationales:

- Many forms of expression have become archaic, while still generally intelligible.
- Other words are obsolete and no longer understood by the common reader.
- The greatest problem is words that are still in constant use but now convey a different meaning from that which they had in 1611.

The NRSV, acclaimed for its modern scholarship, takes into account the more recent availability of early manuscripts, but also continues the process of keeping the language accessible to the reader. The NRSV introduction states that changes were made as warranted on the basis of "accuracy, clarity, euphony, and current English usage." It also recognizes "linguistic sexism arising from the inherent bias of the English language toward the masculine gender, a bias that in the case of the Bible has often restricted or obscured the meaning of the original text," and describes the guidelines by which the text was revised.

It must be kept in mind that language is always part of culture, and that language changes as culture changes. The King James Version of the Bible came from an age in which the grammarian Wilson declared that the "natural" order ought to be preserved in language. By this he meant that the "good man of the house should precede the woman, as the better Horse should precede the graye mare."[3] In 1646 another grammarian, Poole, declared that the masculine gender is more worthy than the feminine.[4] It is clear that the societal values that have changed since the writing of the KJV have warranted the creation of new Bible translations.

The acceptance and use of these newer translations are paralleled in the language of worship. The worship books of denominations are for the most part devoid of thee's and thou's and many other archaic expressions. This has undoubtedly caused some pain for worshipers who had memorized liturgies, but has been accepted overall since most people are willing to admit that a clear understanding of the language of worship is basic to the involvement of participants.

This digression into the change of language in Bible translation and liturgy is relevant in that it sets the stage for the appearance of a hymnal that treats language in a similar way. Of course, this is not to equate a hymnal with Scripture. But the reasons for the change in both instances have much in common, as do some of the methods of revision. The overall result is the possibility in worship for Scripture, liturgy, and hymns to have a feeling of being more closely linked due to a more consistent use of language.

Madeleine Forell Marshall, a scholar of languages and a hymn translator, has spoken directly to the issue of language change and the impact upon hymnody.

> I think that we first should acknowledge that hymns are living texts, not historical artifacts. They are only valuable to the extent that they work for modern singers. Language changes over time. The understanding of the human condition changes over time. Varieties of religious experience familiar in one era are alien to another. Living texts must be adapted or discarded. Hymn texts are not Scripture—but if they were, we note how even Scripture is regularly retranslated, which means altered and adapted, to make sense to each era.[5]

It was within the context of cultural (and linguistic) change that the complex task was begun of finding ways to keep the stories and powerful theological teachings of our heritage of hymn poetry intact, while at the same time discovering images that communicate directly to us today and expand our understanding. How this was done in specific instances is explained later.

The New Century Hymnal is not the first hymnal to deal with the issue of inclusive language. It does, however, represent the most even and consistent approach to language of any hymnal yet published. Rather than choosing to present only *new* hymns in inclusive language, those responsible for the language of this hymnal took the General Synod request for an inclusive hymnal quite literally. Thus hymns of other ages are presented in ways that seek to maintain the theology and beauty of the original, but without some of the biases of the time in which they were written. This hymnal also includes the ethno-cultural diversity of the church and society at large, since for a hymnal to be inclusive, it needs to attempt to reflect the multiracial and multicultural composition of the world in which it is used.

The Process Used

The Hymnal Committee worked from 1990–1994 to accomplish this enormous task. During that time the contents of the hymnal were selected and the way in which the book would be organized was decided. Since the majority of local churches select their scriptures according to the lectionary, a pattern of scripture readings for each Sunday, it was decided that the hymnal would be compatible with the lectionary. That is to say, hymns were selected that would be relevant to the scripture readings for each Sunday. On the basis of conversation with local church leaders, orders for worship were chosen. From the original research that preceded the project, hymns that were essential to large numbers of worshipers were identified. The various tunes commonly used for familiar hymns were reviewed and evaluated.

The next step required was the revision of texts to carry out the intent of the 1977 General Synod action asking for the creation of a hymnal for the church using intentionally inclusive language.

An editorial panel completed the task of the review of each text and monitored the work of the editorial staff and the poets who were engaged to make the revisions. (For further discussion of the process, see the introduction to *The New Century Hymnal*.)

The Theological Demands of Revising Hymns

Inclusive language is not just for the sake of clear understanding in a changing cultural context. There are also important theological principles at stake. The United Church of Christ has spoken very directly to the issue of inclusive language over a period of many years. In November of 1979 *Inclusive Language Guidelines for Use and Study in the United Church of Christ* were adopted by the Executive Council of the denomination and published in 1980. The introduction to this document contains this statement:

> A society in which sexual or racial discrimination is traditional will employ a language in which that bias is reflected. Changes in the language to correct such bias can both reflect changes in the society and at the same time produce such changes. If women and ethnic racial groups are to be acknowledged as full human beings and partners with men and white people in the fullness of Jesus Christ, we must, as a church, confront language bias and as a church act as a continual force for human liberation, salvation, and healing. Change occurs slowly and only through the commitment of the many who begin to demonstrate new vision and new behavior. Such commitment will produce new ways of speaking about the movement of God in history as that power which has liberated and freed us all from the bondage of the past.

The premise of inclusive language has been articulated well by many within the church. But the challenge of implementing change on a large scale, particularly in the process of creating an inclusive-language hymnal, remained uncharted territory to those given the task. Brian Wren, the well-known hymnwriter, theologian, teacher, and poet, has provided what could have been a charge to the poets and editors of *The New Century Hymnal* in this quotation from his book on the language of worship, *What Language Shall I Borrow.*

> Language change is not *all-important:* if it were, then changing language would be all that was needed to change the world. Nor is it *unimportant:* if it were, we could concentrate on doing love and justice, and quit worrying about how we speak of God. To separate language from action is false. Language change is an *essential part of action.* If I cease using racist language I will not thereby end racism. Yet trying out new forms of speech is a necessary part of finding out what I really think. By using nonracist language I also commit myself more deeply than before, even if I can't completely live out my commitment. Language is a public medium. If I use, or abandon, racist or sexist language, or begin to name God anew, I shall open myself to comment and criticism and shall have to explain and defend my usage. It may then be easier than before to act on what I have said.[6]

The editorial panel that was given the task of overseeing the revision of texts for this new hymnal soon discovered the complexity of the task. The many considerations for each and every hymn are impossible to enumerate and describe, but suffice it to say that all hymns became a theological task. One of the reasons is that each hymn brought with it the biases of its time, and to bring a hymn into our time meant looking at it through various lenses. Considerations that were applied to each hymn included:[7]

- Is the hymn in the "memory bank" (that is, hymns where words have been committed to memory by many people)? If so, can the changes be made "invisibly" so that the singer will not be aware of an obvious change? If not, can the hymn be rewritten by a poet in some way that will maintain the style, flow, and theological content?

- Does the hymn contain language that diminishes any

person's full humanity as a consequence of physical ability, human stereotype, family status, or gender?

- Will language for God in this hymn be part of a balance in the final collection of nongendered, feminine, masculine, and other metaphors that build upon and expand our view of God?
- Is the use of the word "Lord" integral to the meaning of the hymn?

- If the hymn speaks of the authority of God, can the paradox between authority and servanthood be maintained (the image of the God who both rules and serves) while using language that is not gender-specific?

- Does the hymn have triumphalist language—that is to say, metaphors and analogies that point toward imposing the authority of a brand of cultural Christianity upon the people of the world?

- Does the hymn have coercive, militaristic language? If it does, can language be found to express the very real struggle against evil using the "weapon" of love?

- Does the hymn have archaic language, an archaic world-view, or archaic theology that can be changed?

- Will the hymns speak to the pluralities of human existence? That is to say, will the collection present, for example, exclusively rural or urban images? Will the collection present only a Eurocentric or North American point of view? Do Christmas carols include images other than those of the cold weather and the snow of the Northern Hemisphere?

- Does the hymn speak in light/dark imagery? If so, can the language be altered to keep an essential biblical or confessional theme without reinforcing racial stereotyping? In this regard, can some hymns give positive and affirming meanings to the word "dark"?

- Does the hymn present theology connected to an outmoded view of the cosmos, such as a three-tiered universe with heaven located up and hell down?

- Does the hymn present stewardship as a matter of manipulating human resources only for human benefit? If so, can it be altered to recognize the possibility of the alignment of human energies to God's purposes?

- Does the hymn promote a "domination" theology of creation in which the human species is always at the summit? Can ways be found to express a sensitivity to the place of humanity within God's design rather than in control over God's design?

This listing gives some idea of the breadth of the considerations given to texts. Although the hymnal committee had given much thought in the selection process and had developed guidelines for language, much of which is distilled in the above listing of guidelines, it became the job of the editorial panel to find a way of revising texts and to apply a final review process to each hymn.

Hymns identified as having language difficulties that were considered to be in the public domain or where the authors were no longer alive were sent to poets along with observations by the panel citing the language of concern, and the poets began the process of submitting drafts of revisions. In the case of living authors, the authors were asked to make the changes themselves, or permission was sought to change the hymns. Among the most difficult were those involving archaic language, since the change of a "thee" or "thy" might entail a considerable reworking of the text. The task would have been easier if each hymn presented only one type of problem. But in many cases, the combination of, for example, archaisms, gendered language, and triumphalism within the same hymn called for a large number of alterations.

This work probably could not have been accomplished by a "scientific" process in which each time a problematic word occurred it was methodically replaced by another. That is not possible with poetry, where each adjustment has to be true to the style and structure of the whole. Nor did it prove feasible that a committee of text revisers could work in a collaborative process around each hymn. Individual poets working on hymns one by one made the task of revision possible. That is because each hymn as a work of art needed the personal attention of a poet sympathetic to the poetical, musical, and theological integrity of the overall text. Some of the very best hymnwriters of this age contributed their skills, each being assigned lists of individual hymns. Hymnwriters who spend their lives writing hymns with the hope that they will be sung for many years understand so well the integrity that they infuse into their own work. Consequently, they respect the work of others given to them to be transformed into language that makes sense for worship today. For these reasons they are best equipped to bring about changes in the hymns of their predecessors. The work was not devoid of struggle and emotion, as all the people involved in the process—poets, editorial panel, and editorial staff—realized they were working with texts that they themselves had memorized and loved.

Inclusive-Language Considerations in One Text

Here is an example of the complexity of considering language revision in a single hymn text.

Joyful, joyful, we adore **thee**, God of glory, **Lord** of love;
Hearts unfold like flowers before **thee**, opening to the sun above,
Melt the clouds of sin and sadness, drive the **dark of doubt** away;
Giver of immortal gladness, fill us with the light of day.

All **thy** works with joy surround **thee**, earth and heaven reflect **thy** rays,
Stars and angels sing around **thee**, center of unbroken praise.
Field and forest, vale and mountain, flowery meadow, flashing sea,
Chanting bird and flowing fountain, call us to rejoice in **thee**.

Thou art giving and forgiving, ever blessing, ever **blest**,
Well-spring of the joy of living, ocean depth of happy rest!
Thou our **Father, Christ our brother**, all who live in love are **thine**;
Teach us how to love each other, lift us to the joy divine.

Mortals join the happy chorus which the morning stars began;
Father love is reigning **o'er** us, **brother love** binds **man to man**.
Ever singing, **march** we onward, **victors** in the midst of strife,
Joyful music leads us sunward in the **triumph** song of life.

All the words that required review according to the various "lenses" shown in the previous section, "The Theological Demands of Revising Hymns," are marked in bold type in this hymn. The underlined words indicate archaic language that needed to be changed.

"Father," "Christ our brother," and "Father love" were reviewed in regard to use of male words for God or Christ; "dark of doubt" was reviewed in regard to use of dark as an negative word; "march" was reviewed in regard to use of militaristic image; and "victors" and "triumph" were reviewed in regard to use of triumphalism. Finally, "man to man" needed to be reviewed as a way to speak of humankind. Although this task would appear to be formidable, singing through the following revision as it appears in *The New Century Hymnal* (#4) should convince one that such changes are possible. The integrity and spirit of the hymn are preserved, and at the same time, the imagery is expanded.

Joyful, joyful, we adore you, God of glory, God of love;
Hearts unfold like flowers before you, opening to the sun above.
Melt the clouds of sin and sadness, drive the storms of doubt away;
Giver of immortal gladness, fill us with the light of day.

All your works with joy surround you, earth and heaven reflect your rays,
Stars and angels sing around you, center of unbroken praise.
Field and forest, vale and mountain, flowery meadow, flashing sea,
Chanting bird and flowing fountain, teach us what our praise should be.

You are giving and forgiving, ever blessing, ever blessed.
Well-spring of the joy of living, ocean depth of happy rest!
Loving Spirit, Father, Mother, all who love belong to you;
Teach us how to love each other, by that love our joy renew.

Mortals join the mighty chorus which the morning stars began;
Boundless love is reigning o'er us, reconciling race and clan.
Ever singing, move we forward, faithful in the midst of strife,
Joyful music leads us onward in the triumph song of life.

To some people the above example might exhibit some categories of language change that seem needless, or that may be dismissed as "political correctness." But this hymnal is neither about "politics" nor "correctness." The language revisions in *The New Century Hymnal* were undertaken so that, as much as is humanly possible, all people would feel fully included as members of the Body of Christ, the Church.

The Practice of Hymn Revision

It might or might not come as a surprise to some people that revising hymns is a long-standing custom. One of the venerable hymnwriters of the eighteenth century, Isaac Watts, was quite comfortable with the practice: "where any unpleasing word is found, he that leads worship may substitute a better; for, blessed be God, we are not confined to the words of any man in our public solemnities."[8]   The   famed   nineteenth-century hymnwriter James Montgomey was an ardent reviser, and speaking of a hymnal he published in 1819 he writes:

> Good Mr. Cotterill and I bestowed a great deal of labor and care on the compilation of that book: clipping, interlining, and remodeling hymns of all sorts, as we thought we could correct the sentiment or improve the expression.

He commented on one of the hymns that he revised:

> I entirely rewrote the first verse of that favorite hymn, commencing: "There is a fountain filled with blood," etc. The words are objectionable as representing a fountain being filled, instead of springing up: I think my version is unexceptionable: "From Calvary's cross a fountain flows, of water and of blood."

Although Montgomery did not want any of his own hymns to be revised, he recognized that this was inevitable: "When I am gone my hymns will, no doubt, be altered to suit the taste of appropriators."[9]

An 1860 commentary on the use of hymns in worship observes:

> [Persons] of poetic genius ought to be stimulated, rather than discouraged, by the thought that posterity will not willingly let [their] songs die; and that, even if they become antiquated in their present form, they will still live in new and fresh

modifications, or become the germs of other and better songs. . . . Was David deterred from giving his hymns to the world, through fear that they would be modified by some future Milton or Montgomery?[10]

Types of Revisions

Any reputable hymnal through the ages has documented changes. Usually this is indicated with the abbreviation "alt." (altered) after the text writer's name to indicate that either the present editors or perhaps some former editors changed the text. Of course, this is not a perfect process, since that would mean tracking each hymn to its original form, and then observing what changes had taken place. The older the hymn, the more likely that through various editions the text has been altered. In reality, vast numbers of hymns have undergone change throughout their lifetimes. Nevertheless, good editors always try to indicate by the use of "alt." that they are aware that a change has been made. In *The New Century Hymnal* the appearance of "alt." indicates exactly this. In many cases it means that the text has been changed by the preparers of this book. In other cases, it indicates that it is known that the source from which it came contained alterations of the text. Sometimes the changes are extensive, and sometimes merely a single word. (The same can apply to the music of the hymn.)

Another category of change is that indicated by "adapt." (adaptation). When "adapt." appears after the writer's name, the expectation is that the text of the hymn contains considerable departures from the original meaning and content, or at least the text is rendered in a remarkably different style.

Translation

A great number of favorite hymns sung in English are actually translations from a hymn originally written in another language. These translations often reflect the theology and outlook of the time period in which they were made as much as they reflect the style and intent of the original.

When the gendered language in *Of the Father's Love Begotten* was examined, the original fourth-century Latin text by Prudentius was consulted. The original reads *"Corde natus ex parentis,"* which means "born from the heart of the parent." There are many existing translations of the hymn, but the one most often seen in hymnals is from 1854 by John Mason Neale, "Of the Father's love begotten." In the nineteenth century the hymn also appeared in English as "Of the father sole begotten," "Born of God the Father's bosom," "Of the Father's will begotten," "Son Eternal of the Father," "Yea! from the Almighty mind He sprung," and "Of the Father's heart begotten." It is interesting to note that only one of these translations uses the word "heart," and in that case designates that it is the father's heart. The doxology stanza that appears in many hymnals was not part of the original text, nor was the refrain "evermore and evermore." [11] It was the choice of the editorial panel to seek a new translation, which appears as *Of the Parent's Heart Begotten* (#118).

One of the most intensive pieces of translation work was *Hail, O Festal Day!*, which involved examination of the Latin texts used in York, England, in the sixteenth century and the original Latin poem by Fortunatus from the sixth century, and then arranging them for use in the space of one hymn (#262) to provide a festival hymn for use at Easter, Pentecost, or Ascension.

Translators were surprised to discover that a favorite hymn, traditionally listed as "Latin, fourteenth century," contained only one stanza of the original Latin hymn. A more complete description of this hymn (#240), *Jesus Christ Is Risen Today*, is given in Appendix B, but let it suffice at this point to say that the entire story of the women who proclaimed the good news of the resurrection was entirely eliminated through the centuries. Through the gift of a new translation, the original story has been restored.

It is fitting that some hymns of the Reformed tradition receive new translations. The new translation from the Joachim Neander German hymn *Sing Praise to God* (#22) shows how fresh, new images appear when rendered by a scholar and poet who lives and speaks in our own time.

In all, 1 French, 15 German, 1 Greek, 1 Hungarian, 1 Japanese, 1 Lakota (Native American), 12 Latin, 12 Spanish, and 2 Swedish hymns received new translations.

Why the emphasis on new translation? We have had access to many of the hymns of earlier times through the work of such hymn translators as Catherine Winkworth, who died in 1878, and John Mason Neale, who died in 1866. These translators served their own time by giving the church the opportunity to sing the hymns in English. But they were translated into words in common use in their own time, incorporating not only the language styles of that time, but also the prevailing biases of society. Unfortunately, since then little has been offered in the way of modern translations. At best, most hymnals in the twentieth century have made alterations to the texts of the translations of the previous century. There is no intent to discredit the faithful work of these scholars, but to ignore the original texts and their authors does not pay them their due. That is to say, just as the traditional hymns of the church were rightly kept alive by way of translation in another era, so do they deserve to be freshly translated today.

Categories of Language Considerations

The remainder of this booklet addresses the various categories of language that were encountered in the process of text review and revision, and some of the methods that were applied. In each category an attempt is made to present some of the rationale for change and the ways in which the revisions were made. It is not the case that each hymn fell entirely and neatly into one of the categories. As was demonstrated in the example above, many of the hymns involved the consideration of several of the language guidelines already mentioned. It also was not the case that a formula could be applied that would solve each language problem in the same way. And finally, it is important to point out that the entire process from start to finish was one of building and learning with the human limitations that this implies, the chief of which is the possibility, indeed the probability, of inconsistencies. Having said this, what follows is an attempt to put into categories the kinds of language treatment that were generally used in the revision of texts.

Archaic Language

The shift of language from archaic expressions to contemporary usages is perhaps the most difficult of all the challenges for poets who are asked to revise hymns. It is much easier in the case of prose and other nonmetered texts. But in hymns, rhythm, meter, stress on syllables, and rhyme scheme all need to be considered when changing, for example, thee's and thy's at the end of lines. Archaic language is not confined to single words. There are phrases, idioms, and sometimes the entire style that inhibit clear understanding to the singer of today. Take for example a phrase such as "If thou but suffer God to guide thee . . . He'll give thee strength, whate'er betide thee."[12] We should not be too quick to assume that a child growing up on the brink of the twenty-first century will be able to discern the meaning from the context. The same might be true for a person whose first language is not English. Or take for instance the phrase "Beneath the cross of Jesus I fain would take my stand," which is solved, fortunately, quite easily by "I gladly take my stand."

It must be pointed out that such changes are not uncommon in other ages. Charles Wesley originally wrote "Hark, how all the welkin rings," but this, as we know, has been altered to "Hark! the herald angels sing." This is only one of the changes made in this carol over the years.[13] (Examples of other hymns are given in Appendix A.)

The poet-revisers have often shown great creativity when faced with rhyming couplets with archaic words at the end. In *Immortal, Invisible* (#1) the two lines

We blossom and flourish as leaves on the tree,
And wither and perish, but naught changeth thee.

18

are treated this way:

> We blossom and flourish as leaves and as flowers,
>
> then wither and perish—but naught dims your powers.

In *Jesus, the Joy of Loving Hearts* (#329) the lines

> Our restless spirits yearn for thee,
>
> Where'er our changeful lot is cast:
>
> Glad when thy gracious smile we see;
>
> Blest when our faith can hold thee fast.

become

> For you our restless spirits yearn,
>
> Where'er our changing lot is cast;
>
> Glad when your smile on us you turn,
>
> blessed, when by faith we hold you fast.

Had all the challenges presented by archaic language been as easily solved, the revisions would be nearly imperceptible. That was not the case, however, and some hymns needed to be considerably reworked. As was pointed out previously, in most instances, the language difficulties that the hymn presented were multiple; that is to say, more than archaic language needed to be revised.

In the movement from archaic to contemporary language in the hymnal it is fair to observe that sometimes more revising might have taken place than was absolutely necessary. In some instances the opportunity was seized by a poet to use the basic form and text of a hymn, but add some issue of more contemporary relevance. But in each and every such instance it was sincerely hoped that these changes would expand rather than limit the imagery of the text, and give the hymn more power to teach in our own time.

Gender of God

When attempting to render a text in inclusive language, one of the basic issues that needs to be considered is that of gendered words referring to God. In Scripture and throughout the ages God has been addressed as Father. Jesus even used the word

"Abba" (which we could translate today as "Daddy"). The word has held an important place in the worship of the church—at baptism, in doxologies, and in private prayer. The trinitarian formula, "Father, Son, and Holy Spirit," is universally familiar in the creeds of the church. But the notion of using only these terms (two of which are male) exclusively—as the only valid names—to speak separately of the three "persons" of the one "essence" runs counter to earlier tradition. The very theologians of the early church who labored to explain the doctrine of the Trinity at the same time consistently denied that God has gender. Rather they argued that God transcends gender, and they freely used both feminine and masculine words in speaking of God.[14] The idea, then, of not using exclusively male images for God, rather than being a modern invention, holds an important place in historic Christian theology. In Hebrew Scriptures (pre-Christian) the use of "father" to refer to God occurs less than a dozen times; the ancient sacred name YHWH spoken by God to Moses occurs around 6,800 times, and yet its true meaning and even its pronunciation are not clear. However this name may be translated, it is not a name that means father; it is generally transliterated as "Yahweh." It has also been rendered as "Jehovah."

"Father" is used to name the first person in the Trinity. It is a name that associates our thoughts with human attributes. And therein lies the problem of language and human thought. To accept the idea that the true nature of God is beyond human comprehension is to understand that names that stand for God do not denote or identify God literally. This is so well expressed in the orthodox Jewish practice of not speaking the name of God, YHWH. This practice underscores a reverence for the awesome mystery of God, so beyond human understanding that to try to contain the essence of God in a word is a sin. At issue is metaphor. Through consistent use a metaphor comes to be thought of as a literal statement. Simply put, if a child listens to the words of worship and hears God referred to time and time again as father, the child may well come to believe that God is indeed a being with all the attributes that the child associates with a father. How can this learning be reconciled with the scriptural concept that we are all "created in the image of God"? If God created both male and female, does that not imply that God must have both attributes? Again, the early theologians agree to the extent that to deny "the womb of God" was considered heresy. [15]

This hymnal balances the gendered metaphors and similes for God, and lessens the number of masculine pronouns and male images for God. It also strives to enrich the vocabulary of worship by using a wide diversity of metaphors from a variety of sources to refer to God. There is no end to the wealth of names to be found in Scripture and ancient hymns and that emerge from the creative minds of modern hymnwriters.

These are but a few of the names used in *The New Century Hymnal* to refer to God: Ancient of Days, Comforter, Creator, Emmanuel, Father, Mother, Father-Mother, Fashioner of spheres, Fount, God, God of Abraham and Sarah, God of mystery, God Most High, Healer, Holy One, Holy Wisdom, Love Eternal, Maker, Messiah, Mystery, Parent, Redeemer, Rock, Root of life, Savior, Shepherd, Source and Goal, Sovereign, Triune Source, Wakantanka (Lakota language for God), Weaver, Word—and there are many more.

Thus worshipers have the opportunity to praise God with a variety of metaphors that by their diversity can expand the images of God and evoke the mystery of God that is "I AM WHO I AM"—and not limited by a single name. All of this is possible while still embracing the trinitarian name(s) of God, and at the same time giving an equally privileged place to feminine metaphor.

Use of Father for God

In *The New Century Hymnal*, God is not addressed exclusively as Father. The approach to language for God is to use gendered language sparingly, and in balance. Thus, although God is called Father, God is also called Mother. If it is possible to do so, balance is achieved in the same hymn. A careful look at many of the hymns that were reviewed indicated that a reference to Father was not necessarily linked to the rest of the text. In other words, Father was used simply as a name for God, but without relation to the metaphorical content of the rest of the text.

An example is the hymn *Great Is Your Faithfulness* (#423) where the original words "O God my Father" do not have a strong relationship to the rest of the hymn, which as a whole speaks about God's creation. Nor is "Father" used as a name for God in the Lamentations passage (3:22–23) that is the origin of the hymn text. Thus, in this instance the name "Father" is not retained and "Creator" is substituted as a name that is linked with the rest of the text. But in hymn 487 God is described as a "father, gently caring," and the rest of the text speaks of the ways in which this parenting care is shown.

"Father" is also used in some instances where it was decided to maintain the traditional words for the Trinity. (For these examples, see the section "Language about the Trinity.")

Balancing Masculine and Feminine Images

Sometimes hymns have been altered to balance male and female metaphors for God. *Father Almighty, Bless Us with Thy Blessing* as revised by a twentieth-century poet now has more balanced metaphors by substituting "Mother of mercy" in the third verse. The poet has also expanded imagery by adding "Eternal God" and "Christ of compassion." In other cases, balance is accomplished without using words that denote gender. In a baptism hymn (#325) the hymnwriter refers to "God your loving parent," making it possible to imagine God as either a mother or a father. In a benediction hymn (#82) it is again up to the singer to choose to think of God as either (or as both) a mother or a father since the poet has God speaking as "I" to "my children": "Go, my children, with my blessing, you are my own." Hymn 451 uses the image "Mother and Father, you are both to me."

A similar idea is suggested by the use of "Father-Mother" as an option in the prayer of Jesus, "Our Father . . ." In the version given as option B of "Prayer of Our Savior" in "Morning Prayer" and "Evening Prayer" in the Orders for Worship, "Father-Mother" is made available as a way of addressing God. The usage of the hyphenated name "Father-Mother" may appear unusual in that no human has one parent who is both father and mother. In fact, the name may serve as a useful metaphor for God for this very reason. "Father-Mother" lets us address God with images of both fatherly and motherly attributes in mind. The hymn *Bring Many Names* (#11) by Brian Wren is a good example of using gender balance and also other varied images to present the many aspects of God who is always more than we can describe. Among the many names are not only "strong mother," "warm father," but also "old, aching God," "young, growing God," and finally "great, living God, never fully known." It might be striking for some to observe how the poet has avoided the societal stereotype of a strong father and a nurturing mother by reversing the attributes.

Use of Mother and Other Feminine Images for God

Just as some hymns use only father images for God, others refer to God only as mother, or in terms of motherhood. Although balance of gendered metaphors has not been attempted within these hymns, they balance each other in the overall book. Some of these are old, some are revised, and some are newly composed. *How Like a Gentle Spirit* (#443) is a recent hymn that reflects imagery from scriptures (Deut. 32:11–12): "God like a mother eagle hovers near on mighty wings of power." The hymn *Mothering God, You Gave Me Birth* (#467) is a new poem, but it is adapted from the writings of Julian of Norwich, a fourteenth-century abbess. In it God, Christ, and Spirit are expressed as a trinity that acts in mothering ways. The use of feminine images for God is not a development of modern times. It has precedent in the Bible:

As a mother comforts her child, so will I comfort you (Isa. 66:13a).

I have kept myself still and restrained myself; now I will cry out like a woman in labor (Isa. 42:14b).

I will fall upon them like a bear robbed of her cubs (Hos. 13:8).

And Jesus lamenting over Jerusalem employs a feminine image:

How often have I desired to gather your children together as a hen gathers her brood under her wings (Matt. 23:37).

The use of feminine images for God is not particularly a product of women writers. In the third century Clement of Alexandria wrote, "And God himself is love; and out of love to us became feminine. In his ineffable essence he is father; in his compassion to us he became mother." In the fourth century Ambrose of Milan (the writer of *O Splendor of God's Glory Bright*, #87), spoke of the womb of the Father. Lists of early Christian writers cited by modern scholars make it clear that both men and women writers frequently used feminine images for God.

Masculine Pronouns for God

The same ideas that are presented in the preceding sections, "Gender of God" and "Use of Father for God," relate to pronouns referring to God. If male pronouns—he, him, his—are used consistently to refer to God, the user may begin to think of God as a male. Because it is not assumed that God is a male being, the hymnal avoids male pronouns, and finds other ways to speak about God without using gender. This is done in a variety of ways, sometimes requiring a shift in the syntax, the use of God a second time, or the use of another word or nongendered pronoun, for example "who" or "whose." In *God Moves in a Mysterious Way* (#412) the pronoun "he" gives way to adjectives or simply the word "God." Thus "his wonders to perform" becomes "great wonders to perform"; "scan his work" becomes "scan God's work"; and "God is his own interpreter, and he will make it plain" is rendered "God is God's own interpreter, whose truth shall be made plain." There is no claim that such adaptation is a perfect equivalent, but it does maintain the beauty and meaning of the original. This is an example of a process applied frequently to speak of God without giving the impression that God is a being with a specific gender.

The same principles are applied to the renditions of the Psalms. Psalm 121 reads in the NRSV this way:

My help comes from the LORD,
> who made heaven and earth.

He will not let your foot be moved;
> he who keeps you will not slumber.

He who keeps Israel
> will neither slumber nor sleep.

The Psalter of *The New Century Hymnal* renders the word "LORD" as "God" ("Yahweh" in the Hebrew manuscripts—I AM THAT I AM) and the pronouns "he" and "him" as "God"; "his" is rendered "God's" (p. 704):

My help comes from God,
> who made heaven and earth.

God will not let your foot be moved;
> God who keeps you will not slumber.

God who keeps Israel
> will neither slumber nor sleep.

The Psalms thus rendered have lost neither their meaning nor sense of adoration. Yet the process has again been applied for the reasons previously cited. In the whole psalter of the NRSV, the occurrences of the pronouns "he," "him," and "his" to refer to God number over 1,000. And it may be pointed out that the use of the masculine pronouns as subjects of verbs was the result of translating the Psalms into English. They do not exist in the original Hebrew texts.

It is difficult to imagine a person reading through the Psalms for the first time as they appear in most English translations and concluding that God does not have male gender. The ease with which one can read and sing through the psalms in the hymnal in their gender-neutral renderings demonstrates that such a shift is possible while still maintaining the original beauty.

25

Gender of Jesus Christ

The hymnal occasionally retains masculine language for the historical Jesus, especially if that is essential in the storytelling sense. Thus when we sing of the baby boy in the manger, we sing "the little Lord Jesus lay down his sweet head" (#124), and we sing of "Jesus our brother"(#138). Male language is also retained in some other hymns that recount events in the life of Jesus:

148 *What Child Is This*—nails, spear shall pierce him through

213 *Hosanna, Loud Hosanna*—To Jesus, who had blessed them close folded to his breast

229 *Were You There*—when they nailed him to the tree

343 *Jesus Took the Bread*—Jesus broke the bread; then he pouredthe wine

347 *Let Us Talents and Tongues Employ*—at his table he set the tone

498 *Jesu, Jesu*—Knelt at the feet of his friends

It is important to note, however, that in most cases hymns in their total message are not simply about the man Jesus of Nazareth, but refer to the resurrected Jesus, the Christ, who is our Sovereign. In such cases, language has been chosen to express the divinity and sovereignty of Christ without portraying Christ in male terms. In other words, when the hymn is clearly about the resurrected Jesus, or Christ, male-oriented language is usually not used.

Likewise, in cases where the pronoun "he" appears throughout the hymn to refer to the raised Christ, the change has been effected by simply writing in "Christ," thus assuring no loss of identity, but again lessening the overall bias toward the masculine identity of the second person of the Trinity. An example of this may be found in *O Spirit of the Living God* (#263) in the fourth stanza. "So shall we know the power of Him who came mankind to save; So shall we rise with Him to life which soars beyond the grave" has been altered to "So shall we know the power of Christ, the strength of love to save, so shall we rise

26

with Christ to life which soars beyond the grave." And in *In Christ There Is No East or West* (#394, 395), "in him no South or North" becomes "in Christ no South or North."

Also, some hymns were changed to the second person to address Christ as "you" instead of "he," which at the same time adds a more intimate expression of personal faith. An example is *We Hail You God's Anointed* (#104). Phrases such as "he shall come down like showers" and "before him on the mountains" are rendered in second person as "you shall come down like showers" and "before you on the mountains."

Why should such emphasis be given to the distinction between the historical Jesus and the Christ of all humanity? The considerations are essentially the same as those regarding language about God. In the same way that male language to describe God is not emphasized, neither is male language referring to Christ. When Paul speaks of Christ in Col. 1:15–20 he cites numerous aspects of Christ's nature: image of the invisible God; firstborn of all creation, before all things, and through whom all things are held together; head of the body, which is the church; the beginning; firstborn from the dead; the one in whom all the fullness of God was pleased to dwell, and through whom all things are reconciled to God, whether in heaven or earth, through the blood of the cross. What is not central to this description is that Christ is a male being. Another perspective is conveyed by Paul in Gal. 3:27–29: "As many of you as were baptized into Christ have clothed yourselves with Christ. There is no longer Jew or Greek, there is no longer slave or free, there is no longer male and female; for all of you are one in Christ Jesus." Many view this passage to mean that Jesus Christ transcends gender and other social or cultural divisions, uniting us as a new body of faith, the church. The theologian Sandra Schneiders puts it simply: "Christ, in contrast to Jesus, is not male, or more exactly, not exclusively male. Christ is quite accurately portrayed as black, old, Gentile, female, Asian, or Polish. Christ is inclusively all the baptized."[16] The fourth-century theologian Gregory of Nazianzus says of Christ, "that which is not assumed is not redeemed." [17] Because redemption is offered to all, Christ has assumed all that we are—man, woman, rich, poor, weak, and strong. This concept parallels the creation, God's creation of humankind in God's own image, both male and female, just as Christ takes on our humanity—all of it—our richness, our poverty, our weakness, our strength, our maleness, and our femaleness. Jesus Christ has assumed all of our humanity. Rendering texts in language that does not give predominance to gender does not diminish this message.

To make sure that this central image is never lost in our worship, this theme of God taking on our humanity, the incarnation, resounds through the hymns of *The New Century Hymnal*. Hymn 209 is an old Latin hymn newly translated: "O Love, how vast . . . that God a human form should take, and mortal be for mortal's sake."An excellent modern example is *O Christ Jesus, Sent from Heaven* (#47) in which all the images refer to God taking human nature. In the breadth of one hymn Christ, the Word made flesh, is sent from heaven, lives with us, washes feet, is crucified, and feeds the church today. Hymn 208 states clearly that Christ who was made flesh and suffered death is the chief cornerstone, the "ground" of faith. These examples typify the great care with which the belief that Jesus Christ is God incarnate has been preserved, while at the same time avoiding the repetitive use of male-gendered language.

This was considered to be the case, for example, with *O Come All You Faithful* (#135). It is true that the hymn is for the event of Jesus' birth, but the refrain of praise most certainly transcends time and space so that we are singing not only to the babe in the manger, but also to the Christ of all ages, the Christ of men and women, rich and poor, weak and strong. Yet the human incarnation of God is not diminished as the hymn states: "Jesus to you shall all glory be given, Word of our God now in flesh appearing." A change such as this may give pause to many who have memorized hymns, especially carols for Christmas, and it is likely that many will continue singing these carols the way they learned them for some time to come.

Still, in keeping with the language of the entire book, even these hymns were altered.

A parenthetical note here may be in order. The editorial panel that worked with poets to revise all the hymns wrestled with many texts and came to the conclusion that to a large degree the integrity of the hymnal would rest on its treatment of language, as much as is humanly possible, in a consistent way. If language is to be made inclusive, then it should be made inclusive throughout. Such consistency may not be easily accepted in cases where memorized language is at play. But the more important issue to all who worked on this hymnal was this: what language will we hand to a generation yet unborn that will guide their singing and learning of faith?

Lord and Sovereign

The word "Lord" presents a challenge when seeking to diminish the number of instances in which God is referred to in a male image. "Lord" has appeared in hymns with great frequency as a name for God and Jesus. The word implies authority, but it also is a word of gender. There was considerable debate after the word "Lord" had been temporarily eliminated from many hymns. In response to a General Synod action recommending the restoration of the word "Lord" in reference to Jesus Christ, the editorial panel reviewed the revisions that had been made in the hymns using guidelines written by the Executive Committee of the United Church Board for Homeland Ministries' Board of Directors.[18]

As a result, "Lord" when referring to Jesus was retained in cases of well-known, memorized hymns, especially when it appeared in the first stanza. This can be seen in "Here, O my Lord, I see you face to face" (#336); "The church's one foundation is Jesus Christ our Lord" (#386); "the little Lord Jesus lay down his sweet head" (#124); "Lord Jesus, who through forty days"(#211); "Joy to the world! the Lord is come" (#132); and "Teach me, O Lord, your holy way" (#465).

29

In some instances, other language considerations prevailed in the decision to leave out the word "Lord." The following story gives an example of such a case. As the hymn *Fairest Lord Jesus* was being discussed, one of the African American members of the hymnal committee remarked, "to the young people in my congregation, fair means fair-skinned." Knowledge that the same German hymn was translated in some hymnals as "Beautiful Savior" prompted a new translation, "Beautiful Jesus, Head of all creation" (#44).

Finally, in some hymns where the word "Lord" was not used in the original language, it was not retained, such as *Joy Dawned Again on Easter Day* (#241): where Neale had translated "the apostles saw their risen Lord" ("Christ" was used in the original Latin), *The New Century Hymnal* uses "the Risen Christ to them appeared."

The hymn *I Greet You, Sure Redeemer* (#251) has an interesting story of changes. "Lord" does not appear in the fifth stanza of the original French text. In Elizabeth L. Smith's translation that appears in Philip Schaff's *Christ in Song*, the words are "Comfort and give us peace, make us so strong and sure." These words were revised for *The Hymnal of the Reformed Church* 1920 as "Come give us peace, make us so strong and sure." But the 1941 *Hymnal* of the Evangelical and Reformed Church changed the text to "Lord, give us peace, and make us calm and sure." *The New Century Hymnal* uses "O dear Redeemer, make us calm and sure."

The overall result of the entire revision process is that the word "Lord" appears with less frequency than in many other hymnals. In the same way this hymnal has dealt with many other gendered words, words have been found to balance and expand images. One approach was to substitute "Sovereign" or some other word for "Lord" that keeps the idea of authority and hierarchy. This may be found in hymns such as hymn 145, "Jesus . . . who is God and Head of all," and hymn 166, "We may not climb the heavenly steeps to bring the Sovereign down." An instance that does not represent the usual way of applying the above processes occurs in *As with Gladness Those of Old* (#159). The new words are "As with joy they hailed its light, leading onward, beaming bright; so, true Morning Star, may we evermore your splendor see" ("Morning Star" replaces "Most gracious Lord").

To those for whom "Lord" is one of the main ways of addressing Jesus, all of the above changes may be unsatisfactory. But the reality is that "Lord" is respected in the hymnal as one of the many valid names used for Jesus Christ. Furthermore, the confession "Jesus Christ is Lord" is not abandoned in the hymnal, but is expanded by the use of alternative images to express the sovereignty of Jesus Christ.

There is not space here to even summarize the diverse opinions about the word "Lord," but the words of the guidelines used by the editorial panel indicate the spirit in which their work of retaining the use of "Lord" was done, with "sensitivity to the fact that the term 'Lord' represents sexism and injustice for some and a historic and meaningful committed relationship for others."

Use of Lord for God

In general, "Lord" is not used in *The New Century Hymnal* as a name for God. It is only used for Jesus Christ. The same process of substitution of nongendered words was the usual way of treating this word. In the case of the psalter, the word "LORD" as it appears in the New Revised Standard Version is often replaced with "God."

The Son of God, the Child of God

A parent would agree that there is no loss of affection in saying "you are my child" instead of saying "you are my daughter" or "my son." In the same way the relationship of Jesus Christ to God as Son of God can also be expressed by saying that Christ is God's own Child. The filial relationship is affirmed and Christ's humanity is not diminished, even though both are expressed in a way that does not emphasize gender. The use of

31

"Child" to refer to Jesus is not a modern invention. The Greek word *pais*, whose meaning is child or offspring, is used to refer to Jesus in Acts 3:13, 26; 4:27, and so on. The NRSV translates *pais* in those passages as "servant," with a footnote: "*Or child.*"

Pais is also used to refer to Jesus in the early Christian writing, 1 Clement (59:2, 3, 4), written around 96–97 C.E. Cyril C. Richardson translated 1 Clement 59:4 as follows:

"Let all the nations realize that you are the only God," That Jesus Christ is your only Child, and "that we are your people and the sheep of your pasture."[19]

Pais is used for Jesus also in the Didache (9:3; 10:2, 3), which dates from the early second century. Didache 9:3 reads:

We thank you, our Father, for the life and knowledge which
you have revealed through Jesus, your child. [20]

Pais also is used to refer to Jesus in the communion prayer of the Liturgy of Hippolytus of the early third century:

We render thanks unto thee, O God, through Thy Beloved Child Jesus Christ, Whom in the last times Thou didst send to us [to be] a Saviour and Redeemer and the Messenger of Thy counsel.[21]

In a very few instances in *The New Century Hymnal* the name "Son" has been replaced with "Child." Hymn 209 cited previously is an example. It concludes with "By Love we have been reconciled: salvation gained through God's own Child." Another example is found in hymn 198 where "Christ the Child of God" replaces "Christ the Son of God." In *O Come, O Come, Emmanuel* (#116), "until the Son of God appear" becomes "until the Child of God appear."

The first line of the hymn *We Hail You God's Anointed* (#104) bears comment in this regard since "We hail you God's anointed, the long-awaited One!" is quite different from the original "Hail to the Lord's anointed, Great David's greater Son!" From the aspect of gender language, it was apparent that three male names, "Lord," "David," and "Son" in the first line needed consideration. "Lord," in this case clearly referring to God, is changed to "God," and "Great David's greater Son" is changed to "the long-awaited One." Although it is true that the explicit allusion to Jesus' descent from David has been lost, "long-awaited One" most certainly expresses the prophecy of the Messiah, as in the words of John, "are you the one who is to come," and the song of the triumphal entry, "the one who comes in the name of God." That same God is the God of Israel and the God of Christians.

Kings, Kingdoms, and Masters

The use of "king" as a metaphor for God has been replaced in some cases by "sovereign," or some other way has been found to eliminate the masculine gender. Hymn 248 is an example. Although the original hymn begins with the words "The King of love my shepherd is," the entire remainder of the hymn is not about a king but about shepherding. Thus, the king of love image was set aside for "Such perfect love my Shepherd shows." This is not a perfect equivalent, since it could be argued that in fact it should have become "The sovereign of love," or the "ruler of love," or the "queen of love" in a subsequent verse for balance. But the reality is that ruler and sovereign would not work poetically (too many syllables), and balancing king with queen does not seem to achieve the desired result. The solution that was found has integrity. God still showers love and all of the shepherd imagery of the twenty-third psalm is intact. In addition, five male pronouns have been removed. The end result is that the same story is told and the same wonderful metaphor for God as the caring shepherd is still powerfully portrayed, without the need to portray the shepherd as a man who is a king.

An example of the use of sovereign as king is found in the hymn *Rejoice, Give Thanks and Sing* (#303). The original Charles Wesley text "Rejoice! the Lord is King! Your Lord and King adore; mortals, give thanks and sing, and triumph evermore" now reads in *The New Century Hymnal*, "Rejoice, give thanks and sing; your Sovereign God adore! For Christ has robbed death's sting and triumphs evermore." In the original, Wesley's use of male language for God is intensified by repetition: Lord-King-Lord-King in the first line. The original phrase, "His kingdom cannot fail, he reigns o'er earth and heaven," has been changed to "Christ Jesus cannot fail to rule both earth and heaven," since in the first instance there is again the possibility of the inference that it is we, the heirs of the kingdom, who cannot fail, when in fact it is Christ who cannot fail. The revision makes clear that it is Christ who triumphs and reigns, giving us cause to rejoice. The alteration has allowed this hymn to be sung smoothly, with its images of authority and awe, but without using male language for God.

"Master" is a masculine word that for some has implications of oppression, as in the expression master-slave. In the case of *O Master, Let Me Walk with Thee* (#503) it is dealt with quite simply by the substitution of "savior"; thus, "O Savior, let me walk with you." In another case, *You Servants of God* (#305), "your Sovereign proclaim" provides a fitting replacement for "your Master proclaim."

Kingdoms of course imply kings, and predominately male authority; but it is not necessary to use "kingdom" if "dominion" can be substituted.[22] The difficulty that arises is that "kingdom" has two syllables and "dominion" has three. Thus, in some cases the equivalent "realm" is used. In hymn 101, *Comfort, Comfort O My People*, "since the realm of God is here" replaces "since the kingdom now is here." "Realm" also appears in newly written hymns: *Enter in the Realm of God* (#615) and *You Are Salt for the Earth, O People* (#181), for example. "Dominion" is used in *Keep Awake* (#112), in the alternate version of the Nicene Creed (#884), in the alternate versions of the Prayer of Our Savior in morning and evening prayer (pages 56 and 60 in the denominational edition; pages 10 and 14 in the ecumenical edition), and in Psalm 145, verses 11, 12, and 13.

Militaristic Language

Occasionally, a hymn describes the struggle against evil in purely military terms. *For All the Saints* (#299) is an example of the modification of text to keep the message but "tone down" the fighting imagery. The original "O may thy soldiers, faithful, true, and bold, fight as the saints who nobly fought of old, and win with them the victor's crown of gold" has been changed to "Still may your people, faithful, true, and bold, live as the saints who nobly fought of old, and share with them a glorious crown of gold." "Thou, Lord, their captain in the well-fought fight" becomes "you, Christ, the hope that put their fears to flight." In the new rendition, the message is clear, but the imagery of war is diminished. Is the message exactly the same? Probably not, but in this new language, Christ is still the leader, there is still struggle and warfare (see stanza 5), and the hope of triumph is still alive. The difference is that Christ is not symbolized as a military leader, and we are not symbolized as soldiers. It is certain that some will lament the loss of these metaphors, but others cannot sing language of such strong military tendency in a world where violence abounds. It might also be noted here that the "blest communion, fellowship divine" was indeed changed for gender reasons, and is replaced by the equally revered expression for the communion of saints, "Ringed by this cloud of witnesses divine."

Triumphalistic Language

As mentioned earlier, triumphalistic language was scrutinized in the revision process. An example is the fourth stanza of the hymn *Rejoice, Give Thanks and Sing* (#303), which has usually been discarded in modern hymnals, probably because it does have truly triumphalistic overtones: "He sits at God's right hand till all his foes submit, and bow to his command, and fall beneath his feet." *The New Century Hymnal* restores this fourth verse, but in hopeful, expectant words more in keeping with the theology of the church at this time: "Rejoice in glorious hope, for Christ the Judge shall come, and take the faithful up to their eternal home. We soon shall hear a heavenly voice above the trumpet's sound, 'Rejoice!' "

Language about the Trinity

The hymnal committee developed a statement concerning the Trinitarian formula:

Where a hymn is clearly trinitarian, Father, Son and Holy Spirit language may be used, but we will consult poets, theologians, and others in order to search for new ways of expressing the Triune God within orthodox parameters. We will use references to the Trinity only when they are part of the essential text.

Recognizing that intense discussion about the language used to express the doctrine of the Trinity is taking place in many denominations, the approach to the use of this language is not monolithic. An examination of trinitarian language in the hymnal should help to show the result.

In the Order for Baptism (page 36 in the denominational edition), the words for the Act of Baptism are "in the name of the Father, and of the Son, and of the Holy Spirit." In hymn 324 the traditional "baptismal formula" is kept in acknowledgment of its validity in the rite of baptism—"O Father, Son, and Holy Ghost." And in what may be the most familiar of traditional Trinity hymns, the entire trinitarian formula is sung in the fourth verse: "Holy Father, Holy Son, Holy Spirit, Three we name you, while in essence truly one, undivided God we claim you." In the ancient evening hymn *Phos Hilaron* (p. 739), one of the hymns of the early church, the names of the persons of the Trinity are retained in the translation: "Immortal Father, heavenly One"; and "Father, Son, and Spirit." It should be pointed out that the first three topics by which the hymns are organized parallel the trinitarian formula: God, Jesus Christ, Holy Spirit (see the table of contents of the hymnal).

Occasionally trinitarian stanzas of hymns have been omitted, especially when they were not integral or original to the hymn. The hymn *All People That on Earth Do Dwell* did not contain the doxological stanza "To Father, Son, and Holy Ghost" in its original 1561 form by William Kethe. It is often the case that doxologies at the ends of a hymn are not part of the original hymn, but are additions in later revisions.[23] The doxological stanza that has appeared with this hymn was composed by John Mason Neale in the nineteenth century. Of course Psalm 100, of which the hymn is a paraphrase, also did not contain these trinitarian words. In this instance, the doxological stanza is omitted in *The New Century Hymnal*.

In some cases, alternate ways of expressing the Trinity were sought by poets. The hymn *Now Thank We All Our God* contained a trinitarian reference which read: "All praise and thanks to God the Father now be given, the Son and him who reigns with them."[24] This has been altered to: "All praise and thanks to God our Maker now be given, To Christ, and Spirit, too, our help in highest heaven, the one eternal God." It is clear that the revision does not name the Trinity in the traditional language of the Nicene formula, but it does what the guideline above suggests—namely, find alternate ways to express praise to the Triune God.

An example of this may be found in the final stanza of hymn 100, *All Praise Be Yours, My God, This Night*: "Praise God who makes, sustains, sets free; one holy God in persons three." But it is not just in hymn *revisions* that these alternate expressions are to be found. The Easter hymn *Alleluia! Alleluia!* (#243, stanza four) sings about the "Triune Majesty" as "God," "Savior," and "Spirit," and these exact words were penned by Christopher Wordsworth in 1872.

Some newer hymns provide excellent examples of the search for alternative language. Jane Parker Huber (#278) begins the four consecutive stanzas of her new hymn with: "Creator God," "Redeemer God," "Sustainer God," and "Great Triune God." In *O Christ Jesus, Sent from Heaven* (#47) by James Crawford, among the many images there is an allusion to the Trinity in the fourth stanza in the words "O Christ Jesus, Father-Mother, Spirit, Triune Source of all." Ruth Duck in *Womb of Life, and Source of Being* (#274) provides many metaphors, including a trilogy of "Womb of life," "Word in flesh," and "Brooding

Spirit." And in the "Service of the Word I" in the Orders for Worship, a benediction is provided in a trinitarian form that balances gender images: "The blessing of the God of Sarah and of Abraham; the blessing of Jesus Christ, born of Mary; the blessing of the Holy Spirit, who broods over us as a mother over her children; be with you all."

Language That Includes Women, Children, and Men

A category of language change that is familiar to most is the use of nongendered language to refer to people. As a matter of fact, this is one aspect of language change for which some groundwork had been laid in recent hymnals and the New Revised Standard Version of the Bible. Throughout *The New Century Hymnal* poets have found creative and expansive ways to change the large volume of male-gendered language to language that includes women and children. In the hymn *Joyful, Joyful, We Adore You* (#4), "reconciling race and clan" replaces "binds man to man." "O brother man, fold to thy heart thy brother" becomes "Children of God, lift hearts to one another" (#533). *God of Grace and God of Glory* (#436) now sings "in the fight to set us free" instead of "set men free." "Strong men and maidens meek" has become "strong souls and spirits meek" in *Rejoice, You Pure in Heart* (#55). *The God of Abraham Praise* (#24) has been given balance by including "The God of Sarah praise." This particular usage, by the way, appears not only in hymns, but in the psalm versions, and in the orders for worship. For example, the blessing (A) in "Service of the Word I" begins, "The blessing of the God of Sarah and of Abraham." These are some of the many ways that both male and female are considered equally as children of God.

Use of the Word "Dark"

The word "dark" has appeared in hymns almost exclusively with negative meaning. Phrases like "the power of darkness" to mean "the power of evil" abound. But "dark" and "darkness" are also associated with skin color, so when we use these words in a negative sense, we also reflect upon those who have dark skin. The same is true with the association of "white" with purity. It is not surprising that Charles Wesley's stanza containing the phrase "wash the Ethiop white" was not included in the Methodist hymnal.[25] In Psalm 51:7 (p. 657), "wash me, and I shall be whiter than snow" becomes "purer than snow." The symbolism of light and dark imagery appears extensively in hymnody, and is deep-rooted in Scripture. It is possible to maintain this contrast and symbolism without using "dark" and "darkness" to denote evil. In the hymns and psalms of *The New Century Hymnal* these words are replaced with other words to denote absence of light, words that simply state the subject of evil, or words that denote the obscuring of light. Thus in *Watcher, Tell Us of the Night* (#103), "darkness takes its flight; doubt and terror are withdrawn" becomes "shadows take their flight." In *Joyful, Joyful, We Adore You* (#4), "Melt the clouds of sin and sadness, drive the dark of doubt away" is changed to "storms of doubt." In *When Morning Gilds the Skies* (#86), the phrase "the powers of darkness fear" is replaced by "let sin and evil fear." Brian Wren uses "darkness" in a positive sense in *Bring Many Names* (#11) in the lines "Great, living God, never fully known, joyful darkness far beyond our seeing."

Language about People's Abilities

The United Church of Christ National Committee on Persons with Disabilities was consulted about the subject of sensitivity to ability. In 1992 this group met and drafted a statement that includes the following:

> As a community of persons with disabilities, we are aware of two realities. There are times when our disabilities have prevented us from being embraced by the church. Sometimes the barriers have been physical, other times they have been attitudinal. We have endeavored to remove these barriers. We are naturally concerned if the words of a hymn are clearly exclusive, implying that the ability to walk, to see, or to talk is a prerequisite to faith. Whenever a change can be made

that reminds us that we are all loved and accepted by God, we affirm that change. At the same time, we are aware that the Bible and many hymns use the language of symbol. We know, for example, that when John Newton wrote in Amazing Grace that "I was blind, but now I see," he was not talking about visual ability, but about seeing with his heart. We know that when Jesus spoke of seeing, he celebrated vision but rejoiced in the perceptive heart. We believe that it would be a mistake to be overly literal, or to automatically exclude every reference to sense or mobility. We are also aware, of course, that what is acceptable to one person is unacceptable to another. . . . We encourage the church to become as loving and accepting as it can be, and to celebrate the joys of the inclusive community in hymns.

This statement represents the starting point for the review of the many hymn texts with references to ability to be included in *The New Century Hymnal*. Throughout the process, the committee made its recommendations, and poets worked to make the necessary revisions.

Words about walking provide an example of language of ability. Hymnbooks are full of "walking" hymns. But "walk" as a metaphor was not invariably excised. In the hymn *O Savior, Let Me Walk with You* (#503) the word remains, since the committee advised that "it is about spiritual walking in the context of bearing, risking, and trusting." Sometimes words about sight were changed, for example, the refrain of *Alas! and Did My Savior Bleed* (#199) has been changed from "At the cross where I first saw the light" to "At the cross where I first found the light." One of the most unique additions was in the hymn *Guide My Feet* (#497), where a suggested extra stanza, "Wheel with me while I run this race," was added in a note to include those in wheelchairs, and as a reminder that not everyone runs races on foot.

Many more examples could be given, but these represent the basic intent of the process. It could be summed up in another quote from one of the letters sent with a group of suggestions.

"The basic point is that the context of the words have a great deal to do with their meaning. If the hymn indicates that one must walk or see in this life to participate in the faith, then a change is warranted. If the hymn indicates that walking or seeing or hearing are things that happen when one is utterly overwhelmed by finding oneself in the presence of God in the hereafter, then a change is not necessary." The difficulty of separating shades of metaphorical usage is quite obvious. It may appear that throughout the book there are inconsistencies, and there probably are, but the work was done within the context that we live in "brokenness," and perfection is achieved only in God's realm. What does matter is that when texts were changed, it was done with the hope of avoiding stereotyping or hurt, and that as an overall result, *The New Century Hymnal* is enriched by another aspect of inclusivity.

Language That Recognizes Varied Human Experience

The hymnal committee recognized that in the past, hymns rarely spoke to some of the "dual" aspects of human existence. They wanted to assure that the collection would present, for example, not just Christmas images of cold weather and snow; not just a Eurocentric or North American point of view; and not only rural, but also urban images. Some of this has been accomplished through the selection of hymns. For Christmas, *Carol Our Christmas* (#141) was chosen for this very reason. The song addresses Christmas in words appropriate for summertime in the southern hemisphere: "Carol the summer, and welcome the Christ Child, warm in our sunshine and sweetness of air." The hymnal as a whole makes possible a more inclusive worldview, and tempers the Eurocentric statement of earlier collections. Occasionally, the language of a hymn was shifted to accommodate this wider view. Hymns that referred to Asia as "the Eastern lands," for example, were altered. The hymn *The Day You Gave Us, God, Is Ended* (#95) replaces "The sun that bids us rest is waking our brethren 'neath the western sky" with "waking our family members far away." And there are instances where new words mention urban life as well as rural. An example of this is in *Heaven and Earth, and Sea and Air* (#566) where the new translation sings of "urban lights and canyons deep, forest, fields, with cows and sheep." A new hymn (#212) begins "O Jesus Christ, may grateful hymns be rising, in every city for your love and care." It was not the intent of the committee that all the images in the book be balanced in this regard, but that there at least be reminders that not everyone's life experience is the same.

Language of Science and Technology

The Science and Technology Working Group of the UCBHM shared its insights with the hymnal committee. This affected both the selection of hymns and the development of language guidelines. Following are the main areas in which the themes of science and technology have been incorporated into *The New Century Hymnal*.

Language of a Three-tiered Universe

Often the hymns of the past, and even hymns written today, speak of our existence in a way that is separate from, if not counter to, our present view of the cosmos. For example, hymns consistently use the language of the three-tiered universe—we are in the middle, God is up, and hell is below. These are only metaphors, but as is always the case, when a single metaphor is used over and over, it becomes a reality in our minds. What is the problem with a metaphor such as God looks "down" on us? This might make sense to some, but to some from the Pacific Rim, it is upside down. For those whose ancient culture focuses on the sea, God is in the depths. Although some of our metaphors indeed come from those whose life was spent looking at the stars, many have spent their lives pondering the depths of the sea.

How does this relate to the language of hymns? There is a need to use a diversity of metaphors to talk about where we and God exist in the cosmos. Of course, we know that we cannot fix God in any one "spot." But we can expand our images about where God "is" in relationship to us. It is amusing to speculate that one of the reasons that so many hymns sing about "God above" is that these words rhyme conveniently with "love" and even "dove," and so our thoughts about God may be somewhat shaped by what rhymes. Users of *The New Century Hymnal* might notice that on occasion, the word "above" may have been changed or augmented to expand the imagery of where God is. A good example of this is *We Worship You, God* (#26), in which "all glorious above" has been changed to "abroad, around, and above." In hymn 6 the nineteenth-century translation "Sing praise to God who reigns above" is replaced by a new translation, "Sing praise to God, our highest good." The number of times that the "location" of God is stated in older (and some newer) texts is significant. We know that hymns function as teaching instruments, and that all people, and especially children, learn fundamental concepts from hymns. Many of these changes simply represent replacing a medieval view of the world with images and language consistent with what children learn daily in school about the universe.

Other Language in an Age of Science and Technology

It is not only in language revision, however, that this hymnal recognizes language of science and technology. Words reflecting everyday life in an age of science and technology rightly appear in some new hymns and translations. In hymn 269 the translator has used modern images to bring alive Paul Gerhardt's seventeenth- century hymn: "Wise and careful, you [God] have counted each electron, all the sands. All-embracing you have bounded space and time in your kind hands." Herbert Stuempfle's new text (#567) speaks clearly to this scientific age in which we find ourselves: "Stars and planets flung in orbit, galaxies that swirl through space, powers hid within the atom, cells that form an infant's face: these, O God, in silence praise you; by your wisdom they are made." In *Creating God, Your Fingers Trace* (#462) Jeffery Rowthorn depicts celestial bodies and the elements of earth praising their creating and sustaining God.

Language of Domination

In traditional hymns about the relationship between humankind and the earth, or nature, there is a central motif. This recurrent theme is portrayed in images of earth and nature as possessions entrusted to people for their care. Human activity is often played out against a backdrop of the lovely scenery of nature. Hymns of this sort, although they may contain beautiful images, by themselves do not speak in terms large enough for a civilization that has learned the power to destroy itself. Catherine Cameron (hymn 556) raises intriguing thoughts about our existence—"[We have] probed the secrets of the atom, yielding unimagined power, facing us with life's destruction or our most triumphant hour." The Science and Technology Working Group encouraged the inclusion of hymns that would use language to expand the view of the relationship of people to their world from simply that of domination and caretaking to that of partnership with and interrelatedness to all of God's creation.

Language Other than English

While no one book could adequately provide resources from every racial/ethnic tradition in the church or the world, *The New Century Hymnal* does offer more than one hundred hymns that are non-European in origin. The selection also represents to a large degree the diversity of cultures and ethnicities embraced within the United Church of Christ and other mainstream denominations in the United States.

One of the linguistic features of this hymnal is that it includes forty-six hymns in languages other than English. Some of these instances are English hymns translated into other languages. A large number of hymns of non-European origin appear with their original language printed first. This practice recognizes that these hymns are gifts to English-speaking culture, and that they are, first of all, hymns with their own cultural origins, made accessible through translation into English.

It was beyond the ability of the editorial panel to review and revise all of the non-English texts according to lenses of inclusive language. But due to the large number of Spanish-language hymns, a great effort was put forth to work with not only the English language translations, but with the original Spanish texts. In fact, it became clear that many of the revisions that were needed in the English translations were as a result of noninclusive language in the original text. In order to resolve this, a working taskforce was established that included bilingual members and a poet. Working together, they first worked to revise the Spanish language text, and then the text was rendered into English language poetry, so that a higher degree of consistency between the Spanish and English texts was created.

New Hymns and New Images

This booklet for the most part has discussed the ways in which texts of older hymns have been transformed to sing in our own time with their original freshness. Much less attention has been paid to new hymns and their new images. Imagery in hymns has been expanded by modern hymnwriters not so much through the development of a new vocabulary, but in the use of everyday words of our times in new ways. One of the most striking and engaging developments is their ability to engage us in a light-hearted expression of our faith as the following examples demonstrate.

In *When Minds and Bodies Meet as One* (#399), Brian Wren uses the poetic rhythm of a jig to express the joy of community:

> When minds and bodies meet as one and find their true affinity,
> we join the dance in God begun and move within the Trinity.

and

> When teamwork serves a common aim, and players move in sympathy,
> the flowing rhythm of the game is beauty in simplicity.

Shirley Erena Murray also employs playful images when writing of the spirit in *Come, Teach Us, Spirit of Our God (#287)*.

> Engage our wits to dance with you, to leap from logic's base,
>
> to capture insight on the wing, to sense your cosmic grace.

When Ruth Duck wrote the hymn *God, We Thank You for Our People (#376)*, she did not hesitate to use words drawn from everyday activity: lessons learned, secrets told, hopes, memories, pranks, stories, and food by loving hands prepared.

Within the six brief stanzas of *God of the sparrow God of the Whale (#32)*, Jarosalav Vajda uses a profusion of images in relation to God: sparrow, whale, swirling stars, creature, earthquake, storm, trumpet blast, rainbow, cross, grave, hungry, sick, prodigal, neighbor, foe, pruning hook, ages, loving heart, and children. Dan Damon uses images of the elephant, eagle, whale, dragonfly, spider, snail, planet, wilderness, rainforest, waterfalls, and trees to engage us in a plea for God's creation in *Pray for the Wilderness (#557)*. Such images from the everyday world are sure to communicate to all of us, and especially children.

These writers can also place before us the fears and sufferings of humanity in contemporary terms. We find allusions to those who are homeless: "When bodies shiver in the night and, weary, wait for morning" (#563). We are reminded of ways of serving our neighbors: "I will hold the Christ-light for you in the shadow of your fear" (#539). The presence of Christ for all the victims of the world is expressed in a hymn that pictures Christ today suffering, imprisoned, scavenging for bread, and begging for crumbs (#587).

Some hymns address racial issues. Hymn 585 speaks of a world in which we can be "torn and pulled apart by hate because our race, our skin is not the same." New verses inspired by *America the Beautiful (#594)* remind us that our people are both "indigenous and immigrant."

Words that spring from our diverse cultures bring still other images to our worship, such as those by the Native American writers Elizabeth Haile and Cecil Corbett in *O God the*

Creator (#291): "the earth is our mother where all things grow" and "gentle deer and the eagle and the mighty buffalo."

Occasionally, new metaphors for God appear as in the first stanza of hymn 398 by Dan Damon: "Shadow and substance, wonder and mystery, spellbinding spinner of atoms and earth; soul of the cosmos, person and energy, source of our being; we sing of your worth." In *By Whatever Name We Call You* (#560) Dosia Carlson calls God the "Fashioner of Spheres," "Mystery," and "All-inclusive One." James Gertmanian describes God as a weaver, "The One whose thread and warp and weft are flesh and earth and air," in *The Weaver's Shuttle Swiftly Flies* (#464). Herman Stuempfle employs the metaphor of a potter in *O God, as with a Potter's Hand* (#550) with some very striking imagery: "And when we seized your choicest work and broke its fragile clay, your hands restored the shattered shards on earth's first Easter day."

All of these examples of new hymns should remind us that when we want to describe the sacred we draw from our own wells of diverse metaphors. In the pluralistic world in which we live, the more ways we have of speaking of ourselves and of God, the more likely we are to gain a better understanding of each other, and of the many ways we have of praising God.

A Word about Perfect Language

God is perfect. Human beings are not, and neither is the language that we use to speak of God. The real danger lies in making idols of the images—the words—we use to address God, thus mistaking these words for the essence of God. We all have fallen short of God's glory, and so do the words we use to speak of God. Still, in our zeal to know God and to praise God, we use the images we have been given and those we create. If we seek to expand those images, we reach toward the possibility of closer relationship. If we seek to limit our language to single formulas, we run the risk of our images of God, and thus our relationship with God, becoming static and tied only to the past. This is at the heart of the issue of language change. The

47

tension of the language in *The New Century Hymnal* is that it does preserve traditional expressions, at the same time allowing new expressions, and it includes both the old and the new in language free from biases that many find to be exclusive. Throughout, the goal is not to achieve the perfect or ultimate version, but to make the hymns live in our own time to be passed into the hands of coming generations, for their use and adaptation.

APPENDIX A
THE WAY IT USED TO BE

Texts of hymns change from time to time and age to age, even some of the most familiar. Following are some examples.

Silent Night

While some may assume that the English version of "Silent Night" (which is a translation from the German, "Stille Nacht") has always existed as we know it today, that is not the case. *The Evangelical Hymnal*, St. Louis, 1917, includes this version:

Holy night, peaceful night!
Through the darkness beams a light
There, where they sweet vigils keep
O'er the Babe in silent sleep,
Resting in heavenly peace,
Resting in heavenly peace.

Those brought up on *The Hymnal of the Reformed Church*, 1920, will remember almost the same words (except for "yonder" instead of "there" and "the Babe who, in silent sleep, rests"). The *Pilgrim Hymnal* of 1935 starts out "Silent night, holy night," but continues, "All is dark, save the light," and then proceeds the same as the Reformed version, "Yonder, where they . . . ." An even earlier version from the *Christian Hymnbook*, Cincinnati, 1865, begins: "Silent night! Hallowed night, Land and deep . . . ."

Faith of our fathers

This well-known hymn is no longer sung in its original form either. The author, Frederick W. Faber, was an English Roman Catholic who wrote this hymn with the political-religious mission of returning the Church of England to Roman rule. The "fathers" were the Catholic priests who were subject to persecution under Queen Elizabeth I. Two versions were published, one for Ireland, and one for England.

St. 1 (Irish version)
Faith of our fathers living still,
In spite of dungeon, fire and sword,
How Ireland's heart beats proud with joy,
Whene'er we hear that glorious word.

St. 3 (English version)
> Faith of our fathers! Mary's prayers
> shall win our country back to thee;
> and through the truth that comes from God
> England shall then indeed be free.

Hark! the herald angels sing

Charles Wesley's familiar Christmas hymn did not originally open with those seemingly timeless words. Stanza 1 began:

> Hark, how all the welkin rings
>
> "Glory to the King of kings!"

The second stanza was different as well. The last two lines of that stanza originally appeared in Wesley's 1739 version as:

> universal nature say,
>
> "Christ the Lord is born today!"

They were changed as early as 1760 in Martin Madan's *Collection of Psalms and Hymns* to the version most know today:

> With the angelic host proclaim,
> "Christ is born in Bethlehem!"

Alas! and did my Savior bleed

The original version of this hymn by Isaac Watts contained several words and phrases that have been changed by editors to reflect more modern usage and sensibilities.

Stanza 1, line 4 was altered from:

> **For such a worm as** I to the more acceptable **For sinners such as I.**

Stanza 3, line 3 has been the object of some theological controversy:

> **When God, the Mighty Maker, died**

was changed in some hymnals to clearly allude to the crucifixion of Jesus with these words:

> **When Christ, the great Redeemer, died**

Other words in this hymn that have been changed over time, include: "crimes" to "sins" and "groaned upon" to "suffered on" (st. 2).

(This appendix is reprinted from *Discovering The New Century Hymnal: A Discussion Guide for Church Musicians, Pastors, and Congregations*, The Pilgrim Press, Cleveland, Ohio, 1995, Appendix C.)

APPENDIX B
HYMNS IN TRANSITION:
"JESUS CHRIST IS RISEN TODAY!"

This favorite Easter hymn has a history dating at least to the fourteenth century. It had eleven stanzas, beginning with:

> Surrexit Christus hodie humano pro solamine, Alleluia.
> (Jesus Christ arose today for human solace, Alleluia.)

The familiar form that has been sung in the twentieth century is from various sources, with only the first stanza having any relationship to the original Latin. The translation of that verse comes from *Lyra Davidica*, London, 1708, a collection of new songs and translations from German and Latin:

> Jesus Christ is risen today, Alleluia.
> Our triumphant holy day,
> Who did once upon the Cross
> Suffer to redeem our loss.

The other familiar verses were added in the eighteenth century, and have little, if any, relationship to the original Latin hymn:

> St. 2, beginning: Hymns of praise now let us sing . . .
> St. 3, beginning: But the pains which he endured . . .

These are from Arnold's *Compleat Psalmodist*, second edition, 1749. Some hymnals carry still another stanza, created by Charles Wesley in 1740 (again, with no connection to the original Latin):

> beginning: Sing we to our God above . . .

But what of the original Latin hymn of which only one stanza survived? What was the story it told? The rest of this remarkable text tells the story of the women bearing spices to the tomb, meeting the angel, and running to tell the good news of the Resurrection. It is a drama filled with joy—a poetic narrative for Easter. It was not uncommon in the medieval church for the story to be acted out, and it is very possible that this great storytelling narrative hymn was used for just that purpose, as worshipers reenacted the scripture while they sang this hymn in a garden outside the church on Easter morning.

The decision to restore this ancient text to hymnody is an example of several such efforts in *The New Century Hymnal* whereby early hymns have been translated from German and Latin and put into fresh English poetry. *The New Century Hymnal* English version follows very closely the original Latin hymn, giving us not only a treasure intact from early church worship, but also the beautiful telling of the story of the women, which earlier revisers chose to drop.

(This appendix is reprinted from *Discovering The New Century Hymnal: A Discussion Guide for Church Musicians, Pastors, and Congregations*, The Pilgrim Press, Cleveland, Ohio, 1995, Appendix A

Notes

1. Ninth General Synod of the United Church of Christ (73-GS-41).

2. Eleventh General Synod of the United Church of Christ (77–GS–17).

3. As quoted in "Language Thought and Social Justice," The Task Force on Educational Strategies for an Inclusive Church, National Council of the Churches of Christ in the U.S.A., New York, 1986, 1.

4. Ibid.

5. Madeleine Forell Marshall, *Common Hymnsense* (Chicago: G.I.A. Publications, 1995), 10.

6. Brian Wren, *What Language Shall I Borrow? God-Talk in Worship: A Male Response to Feminist Theology* (New York: Crossroad, 1991), 82.

7. Adapted from the working guidelines for language of the Hymnal Committee.

8. From Watt's preface to his fourth volume of hymns as quoted in Austin Phelps and Edward A. Park, professors at Andover, and Daniel I Furber, pastor at Newton *Hymns and Choirs: or, The Matter and the Manner of the Service of Song in the House of the Lord,* (Andover, Mass.: Warren F. Draper, 1860), 145.

9. Ibid., 145.

10. Ibid., 144.

11. John Julian, *A Dictionary of Hymnology* (New York: Dover Publications, rev. 1907), 1: 276.

12. For a new version, see hymn 410 in *The New Century Hymnal.*

13. John Julian, *A Dictionary of Hymnology*, 1:487.

14. Jaraslov Pelikan, *Christianity and Classical Culture* (New Haven: Yale University Press, 1993), 87, 88.

15. See Jürgen Moltmann, "The Motherly Father: Is Trinitarian Patripassionism Replacing Theological Patriarchalism?," *Consilium*, 1981, no. 143:51–56.

16. Sandra M. Schneiders, *Women and the Word: The Gender of God in the New Testament and the Spirituality of Women* (Mahwah, N.J.: Paulist Press, 1986), 54.

17. Ibid.

18. The following is taken from the report of the Executive Committee of the United Church Board of Directors to the Executive Council of the General Synod.

The members of the Executive Committee [of the UCBHM] reviewed the goals, history, and status of the hymnal, and the Synod action and its implications. Foremost in the discussions of the Executive Committee were:

• The covenantal responsibility of the UCBHM for a task entrusted to it by the General Synod.

• The goal of publishing for the UCC "a fully inclusive" hymnal as specified in the action of the Tenth General Synod and authorized by the Seventeenth General Synod.

• The historical and personal significance of the term "Lord" for many, as expressed in the request of the Nineteenth General Synod.

• The difficulties with the term "Lord" for many others, as expressed in the responses of UCC churches and members during the development of the hymnal and in the deliberations of the Synod.

In response to the action of General Synod on July 19, 1993, and with extraordinary sensitivity to the fact that the term "Lord" represents sexism and injustice for some and a historic and meaningful committed relationship to Jesus for others, the Executive Committee of the UCBHM Board of Directors establishes the following guidelines for the Editorial Panel in making changes in hymns in *The New Century Hymnal* where "Lord" has been replaced by "Christ."

1) That changes be made only where they will not jeopardize the 1995 publication date and budget commitments, and

2) That special consideration will be given to memory bank hymns, and

3) That consideration be given to restoring the word "Lord" if the original hymn is not compromised by other language or images, and

4) That the original language of the poets be respected when the word "Lord" was added to a hymn by translation.

19. Cyril C. Richardson, *Early Christian Fathers* (Philadelphia: Westminster Press, 1953), 71.

20. Ibid., 175.

21. See Bard Thompson, *Liturgies of the Western Church*, (Philadelphia: Fortress Press, 1961), 20.

22. An excellent explanation of the semantics of the word dominion written by Burton H. Throckmorton Jr. may be found in *Prism* (Spring 1987): 40, n.1. In brief it states that in the Greek scriptures Jesus speaks of the *basileia* of God. That has been translated in English as "kingdom." Throckmorton suggests that "dominion" is more appropriate since it connotes the idea of "rule"(the exercise of authority) and "realm"(the place that is ruled) as does *basileia*, whereas "kingdom" denotes only the realm.

23. In the fourth century Ambrose of Milan attached a doxology to the end of his hymns as a strong statement of orthodoxy in his dispute with the Arians.

In the early nineteenth century the Oxford Movement in England, which had great interest in returning to medieval hymns, resumed the practice of attaching doxologies to the ends of hymns, including preexisting hymns that did not have doxologies. For a more complete discussion, see Erick Routley, *Church Music and the Christian Faith* (Carol Stream, Ill.: Agape, 1978), 97–98.

24. In German, "Preis sei Gott, dem Vater und dem Sohne und dem, der beiden gleich."

25. In *The United Methodist Hymnal* (The United Methodist Publishing House, 1989), the entire hymn, "Glory to God, and Praise, and Love, " is printed, all 18 stanzas, in its original form. But the following stanza was rightfully dropped:

Awake from guilty Nature's Sleep,
And CHRIST shall give you Light,
Cast all your Sins into the Deep,
And wash the Ethiop white.

(It is from this original hymn that the well-known hymn "O for a Thousand Tongues" was derived by using stanzas 7, 8, 9, and 1, in that order.)

www.ingramcontent.com/pod-product-compliance
Lightning Source LLC
LaVergne TN
LVHW021624080426
835510LV00019B/2748